Babies Have the Right

Abortion Is a Human Rights Violation

Ellie Centers

BABIES HAVE THE RIGHT

ABORTION IS A HUMAN RIGHTS VIOLATION

ELLIE CENTERS

Babies Have the Right:
Abortion Is a Human Rights Violation

Published October 2017

ISBN-13: 978-1978018365
ISBN-10: 1978018363

To the family of
Ellie Centers

CONTENTS

FOREWORD

On Wednesday, January 11, 2017, I stood before a classroom full of students at Valor Christian College in Columbus, Ohio for the opening session of the *Marriage and Family* class that I teach. After casting the vision for the course, I proceeded to introduce several options available to the students for writing their final paper. One of those options was to write a paper with the suggested title, "A Redemptive Response to the Issue of Abortion." In an attempt to encourage them with the project, I said, "For some of you, the paper you are about to write will be the start of something great. For you preachers in the room, it may be the start of a sermon series. For others, it may be the start of a book that will someday be published."

Ellie Centers was one of my students in that class. None of us could have known on that day that Ellie would not have the opportunity to complete the assignment. Having barely started the semester, on January 31, we all received the shocking news that this lovely young woman had passed away. Our hearts were broken, and even now, I still sense the sorrow of the loss.

On the day before the funeral, Professor Scott Fleming and I delivered Ellie's personal belongings to her parents in Morrow, Ohio. Before carrying the items into the house, we sat with the family for a while just to talk. It was then that I learned from Ellie's parents that she had been talking about writing her "Abortion" paper for my class only a few days prior to her passing. They proceeded to tell me that Ellie was passionate about the topic in her high school years.

It was then that I asked, "Do you have anything that she ever wrote in high school about abortion?"

Within moments they placed in my hands a paper that Ellie had written in high school, entitled, "Babies Have the Right: Abortion is a Human Rights Violation."

I carefully glanced over the paper page by page. "You know, I told my students that one day their work on this topic may be published. Would you be okay with me publishing this?" They agreed to let me publish it.

The next day during the funeral, I heard a number of testimonies from family and friends reporting that Ellie had hoped to be a voice for the unborn. She was devoted to the pro-life message. That was all I needed to hear to confirm that publishing Ellie's paper was the right thing to do.

Chapter one of this book is entirely the work of Ellie Centers, written while she was a high school student. A little editorial work has been applied, but nothing in the content of her message has been changed. It is my hope that the release of this publication will serve as a way to help perpetuate the life-message of Ellie Centers.

J. Randolph Turpin, D.Min.
October 5, 2017

1

BABIES HAVE THE RIGHT

Abortion has become too common in the United States. One study has revealed that "twenty-one percent of all pregnancies (excluding miscarriages) end in abortion" ("Induced Abortion in the United States" 1). Over one million abortions occur each year.

Twenty years ago, a young woman at the age of nineteen accidentally got pregnant. She decided to have an abortion, seeing that she did not want her family, church or friends to find out. As far as the procedure was concerned, it went well, and later in life, she had no trouble starting a family when she was ready. However, now at the age of thirty-nine, being closer to God, she feels convicted and regrets having the abortion. She often wonders about her baby and what he or she would have been like, looked like and laughed like.

The endless murdering of babies is out of control. Consider the millions who have been aborted. These helpless children never had a voice, and they never had a chance at living life.

The legalization of abortion should be terminated, because as a country that guarantees life, liberty and the pursuit of happiness, the United States is not keeping that promise. Abortion is a human rights violation, because a fetus—an unborn child—is a real human. "Fetus" is a developmental stage in human life. An unborn child is alive; there is evidence of life in the unborn children. There are always other options to preserve life.

First of all, no matter what stage of life the baby is in, the fetus is a human, too. Even though they may be slightly different, a fetus is still a person. No person should have to die for any reason. As stated in an article entitled, "20 Abortion Facts,"

> Like toddler and adolescent, the terms 'embryo' and 'fetus' do not refer to nonhuman, but to humans at particular stages of development. Human beings inside the womb are smaller, less developed and more independent than human beings outside the womb. These are differences of degree, not differences of kind ("20 Abortion Facts" 1-2).

A person might call their mother an adult, or their son a teenager, but it is not legal to kill them, simply because they are unwanted. Abortion kills a human, not an alien, not an object that is not alive, but a living human. Aborted babies are human beings, they are just not strong enough to be independent yet.

Gallup polls determined that 60% of people think an abortion should be legal in the first trimester, while 60% think it should be illegal in the second trimester, and the amount of people who think abortion should be illegal in the third trimester is 80%, a 20% increase from the second trimester (Gallup Poll 8).

In the end, most people think a fetus is less human in the first three months than in the last six months. All humans are equal, it does not matter whether they are extremely old or extremely young, everybody deserves the right to live a life as long as they can, and taking anyone's life should not be allowed. It is no secret that a majority of America agrees that a fetus is not a living human. However, not only are fetuses humans, there is evidence to prove that they show the characteristics necessary for life.

Next, the babies being aborted show signs of life, because these signs begin at conception. The child shows signs of life in the womb, whether doctors like it or not, it's a fact. Planned

Parenthood says, "In later second-trimester procedures, you may also need a shot through your abdomen to make sure the fetus' heart stops before the procedure begins" ("In-Clinic Abortion Procedures" 3).[1]

If there is a heartbeat, why isn't abortion considered murder? If it is illegal to intentionally stop a person's heart who is outside the womb, it should be illegal to intentionally stop a defenseless heart inside the womb. The baby has no way to defend itself, seeing as it isn't fully developed. He or she cannot show emotion yet, although they can feel distress and pain. It is also true that brainwaves and heartbeats are present from the time the embryo is developed. The article, "20 Abortion Facts," further states,

> "What do we call it when a person no longer has a heartbeat or brainwaves? Death. It's a scientific fact that life begins at conception, but even more obvious; what should we call it when there is a heartbeat and there are

---

[1] Editor's note: In an apparent attempt to soften the negative impact of this original wording, Planned Parenthood has revised the text to read, "In later second-trimester procedures, you may also need a shot through your abdomen to make sure there is *fetal demise* [italics added] before the procedure begins." "In-Clinic Abortion," Planned Parenthood, https:// www.plannedparenthood.org/ planned-parenthood-illinois/patient-resources/abortion-services/clinic-abortion.

brainwaves? Life. It is an indisputable fact that each and every legal surgical abortion in America today stops a beating heart and stops already measurable brain waves" ("20 Abortion Facts" 3).

Thus, it is a proven fact that a baby in the womb has a heart and a brain, which are the two main factors that make living organisms, by definition, living. Even though a young fetus many not be able to live on their own, killing them would be like killing anybody who has to rely on a form of medicine or machine to live. Without insulin, diabetics would die. Without an inhaler, some asthmatics would die. It is morally wrong to deny them treatment and allow them to suffer. If a baby cannot survive outside the womb, it is not right to strip them of the safety, sanctity and life provided by taking them out and allowing them to cease living. Abortion is a violation of life for a baby, and even though it may seem like an easy way to escape parenthood, there are more ways to not raise a child, while also saving its life.

Finally and most importantly, abortion is a violation of human rights. There are options other than the death of an innocent child, if the parent(s) are not prepared to raise a child. First of all, contraception is easy and accessible. Planned parenthood explains, "Birth control is an important and common concern for many women.... Talk with your health care provider about getting a birth control method that's right for you" ("In-Clinic Abortion Procedures" 6). If birth control is used while women are sexually active, it is almost promised that they will not get pregnant. With this comes the security of knowing that if they do not get pregnant, they will not have to worry about a child or the pain of getting an abortion.

If the irresponsibility of the mother is the reason she is pregnant, the child should not have to pay for her mistakes. Also, with the laws in place that allow abortion, people are more able to manipulate the system and not use the other options.

In February of 2014, this tragic story was reported: "This winter, John Welden, formerly a pre-med student from a privileged background sits in prison serving a nearly 14-year federal sentence of tricking Lee [his girlfriend] into taking an abortion pill," causing her to miscarry and lose the child. This is a sad story of a first-time mommy-to-be losing her child because of selfishness and lack of communication ("Woman Tricked into Abortion" 1-3). Essentially, if Welden had not had access to the medical abortion drug, he would not have tricked her, and the baby would be alive. They could have put the baby up for adoption, he would not have tricked her, and the baby would be alive. They could have put the baby up for adoption, given it up to a family member, or even split up. The child, already named "Memphis," would not be deceased today. If the abortion drugs were not so accessible, lives would not be lost so easily and carelessly. Abortion is not necessary (the death of an innocent child is not worth the loss), if that precious life can be saved.

Abortion takes away a human's rights because the babies are still developing as humans; fetuses are alive and living, and there are alternatives to abortion so that no human has to die.

Abortion is a widespread problem, not just in the United States, but everywhere in the world. Millions of babies are dying every day at the request of people who should love them more than life itself. If abortion continues, the world will suffer. Whether the abortions are taking place because of discrimination or unpreparedness, populations will deplete.

In the Bible, regarding judgment that God brought because of Manasseh's sins, 2 Kings 24:4 states, "And also for the innocent blood that he shed: for he filled Jerusalem with innocent blood, and the Lord was not willing to pardon." Judgment came because of the shedding of *innocent* blood. Babies are innocent; they have no defense. It is a sin to kill innocent people, yet it is legal. The government is supposed to help us, not allow us to condemn ourselves. We are "One nation, under God," and when God is ignored, structure and peace begin to disappear.

Abortion is not solving any problems, such as the loss of freedom for soon-to-be mothers, it only causes problems, and the only solution is to stop abortion entirely. No longer allowing doctors to legally perform abortion will decrease the abortion rate massively. If the babies can't fight for themselves, who will?

2

EDITORIAL ADDENDUM
SCRIPTURES TO CONSIDER

The Bible has much to say to affirm the sacredness of human life. The following passages bring particular focus to the value of a life while yet in the mother's womb.

Psalm 139:13-16

13 You brought my inner parts into being;
You wove me in my mother's womb.
14 I will praise you, for You made me with
fear and wonder;
marvelous are Your works,
and You know me completely.
15 My frame was not hidden from You
when I was made in secret,
and intricately put together in the lowest
parts of the earth.
16 Your eyes saw me unformed,
yet in Your book all my days were written,
before any of them came into being.

Jeremiah 1:5

5 "Before I formed you in the womb
I knew you;
and before you were born I sanctified you,
and I ordained you a prophet to the
nations."

Psalm 127:3-5

3 Look, children are a gift of the Lord,
and the fruit of the womb is a reward.
4 As arrows in the hand of a mighty
warrior,
so are the children of one's youth.
5 Happy is the man
who has his quiver full of them;
he shall not be ashamed
when he speaks with the enemies at the
gate.

Genesis 1:27

27 So God created man in His own image;
in the image of God He created him;
male and female He created them.

Psalm 22:10

10 I was cast on You from birth;
You are my God from my mother's womb.

Isaiah 49:15

15 Can a woman forget her nursing child,
and have no compassion on the son of her
womb?
Even these may forget,
yet I will not forget.

For women who have had abortions, there is hope.
God is ready to forgive and heal.

Psalm 32:5

5 I acknowledged my sin to You,
and my iniquity I did not conceal.
I said, "I will confess my transgressions to
the Lord,"
and You forgave the iniquity of my sin.
Selah

1 John 1:9

9 If we confess our sins, He is faithful and
just to forgive us our sins and cleanse us
from all unrighteousness.

Romans 8:1

1 There is therefore now no condemnation
for those who are in Christ Jesus, who
walk not according to the flesh, but
according to the Spirit.

Psalm 147:3

3 He heals the broken in heart,
and binds up their wounds.

24

3

Help Is Available

Are you pregnant and need help? There are many agencies that genuinely care about you and the life of your baby. They can help. A few of those agencies are listed below. (The publisher does not officially endorse any of these services. You are encouraged to carefully select the agency that you call.)

National Life Center
Call: (800) 848-LOVE

Bethany
Call: (800) 238-4269

Birthright International
Call: (800) 550-4900

Liberty Godparent Maternity Home
Call: (434) 845-3466

The Women's Clinic of Columbus
Call: (614) 237-2000

Works Cited

The following list of cited works was compiled after the death of the author and during the editorial process. Some sources could not be precisely identified.

"20 Abortion Facts." HisWay1.com Inspirational Website. http://www.hisway1.com/abortion-facts.

Gallup Poll. The specific poll referenced in the author's work could not be identified.

"In-Clinic Abortion Procedures." At the time of publication, the current equivalent to this source is "In-Clinic Abortion." Planned Parenthood. https://www. plannedparenthood. org/ planned- parenthood- illinois/ patient-resources/abortion-services/clinic-abortion.

"Induced Abortions in the United States." *Fact Sheet*, September 2016. Guttmacher Institute, 2016.

"Woman Tricked into Abortion." The original article cannot be located. The same account is reported in "Florida woman tricked into abortion seeks fetal protection laws." Reuters, February 19, 2014. http:// www.reuters.com/ article/us-usa-florida-abortion/florida-woman-tricked-into-abortion-seeks-fetal-protection-laws-idUSBREA1J00R20140220

To order more copies of
Babies Have the Right
go to…

DECLARATIONPRESS.COM